Prema
November, 1990

ENDANGERED ANIMALS

Publications, International, Ltd.

CONTENTS

Louis Weber, C.E.O.
Publications International, Ltd.
7373 N. Cicero Avenue
Lincolnwood, IL 60646

Permission is never granted for commercial purposes.

Manufactured in Yugoslavia
h g f e d c b a

ISBN: 0-88176-831-6

Library of Congress Catalog Card Number: 90-60048

Contributing Author: Lynn Orr Miller
Consultant: Richard Block
Mr. Block is Director of Public Programs for the World Wildlife Fund. He has a bachelor's degree in environmental studies and a master's degree in natural resources. He worked as a curator at Zoo Atlanta and the Kansas City Zoo before he joined the staff of the World Wildlife Fund in 1987.

PHOTO CREDITS:
Animals Animals: Anthony Bannister: 6; M.A. Chappell: 53; John Chellman: 10, 32; Margot Conte: 65; E.R. Degginger: 12-13; Adrienne T. Gibson: 80; George H.H. Huey: 81; Richard Kolar: 73, 74-75; Zig Leszcynski: 8-9, 38-39, 57; Terry G. Murphy: 70-71; Patti Murray: 20; Ralph A. Reinhold: 5, 50-51, 58-59; Ray Richardson: 92; J.H. Robinson: 44; Leonard Lee Rue III: 62-63; Stouffer Prod. Ltd.: 61; Jim Tuten: 11, 26-27, 56; Fred Whitehead: 85, 86-87; Harold E. Wilson: 60; Bruce Coleman Inc.: Karl Ammann: 14, 28, 29; Erwin and Peggy Bauer: 88; Wolfgang Bayer: 7, 54-55; E.R. Degginger: 52; Nicholas DeVore III: 15; Kenneth W. Fink: 21, 22-23, 89, 90-91; Jeff Foott: 94-95; Keith Gunnar: 36; G. Harrison: 84; M.P. Kahl: 30-31; Wayne Lankinen: 48, 64; Dotte Larsen: 72; Wendell Metzen: 78-79; Diana Rogers: 24; Leonard Lee Rue III: 49; Norman Owen Tomalin: 68; Rod Williams: 37; Ellis Wildlife Collection: 34-35; Gerry Ellis: 16-17, 18-19, 45, 69; Chris Huss: 82-83; Tom Stack & Assoc.: Dominique Braud: 25; Jeff Foott: 40, 41; Joe McDonald: 66-67; M. Timothy O'Keefe: 76, 77; Brian Parker: 93; Kevin Schafer: 33; U.S. Fish & Wildlife Service: Dean Biggers: 42-43; John Oberheur: 46-47.
Front Cover: Animals Animals. Back Flap: Animals Animals: Michael Dick.

INTRODUCTION

Have you ever looked at dinosaur bones in a museum and wondered what must have happened to these giant beasts? How could such powerful, fierce-looking creatures have disappeared from the face of the earth? It's a fascinating mystery, one that scientists have been trying to solve for years. But there are more urgent mysteries that need solving, too. These mysteries concern the many animal species that are on the verge of disappearing today. People all over the world are looking for clues. They are trying to discover why these animals are vanishing. And they are working hard to solve the puzzle of how people and animals can share this planet.

People were not around yet when the dinosaurs disappeared. So we can't take the blame for their fate. Theirs was a natural extinction—a disappearance caused by natural changes. But since people have been on earth, more and more animal species have been wiped out. And, unfortunately, people are responsible for driving most of them into extinction. Today, scientists estimate that one out of every ten species of animals and plants—that's more than a million species total—are in danger of disappearing. In the United States alone, more than 270 animals are, or may soon be, in danger of extinction. And that number rises every year.

Why are all these animals so close to disappearing? There are many causes, but the leading one is loss of habitat. In other words, the natural areas where these animals live, eat, and raise their young, are disappearing. As the number of people in the world increases, more land is needed for building homes and raising crops and cattle. As people move into these natural areas, they cut down trees, mine for minerals, fill in swamps, and do other things that destroy the homes and food sources of many animals.

Unregulated hunting has also put many creatures in jeopardy. Sometimes the animals are hunted by people for food. But, as you will see, many more are killed to satisfy the human demand for "animal souvenirs" and folk medicines. Sometimes, animals are killed when they attack cattle or eat crops being raised by humans. Still others die when they eat food that contains chemicals used to kill weeds or insects.

Fortunately, more and more people are becoming aware of how human carelessness is harming the many creatures that share our planet. They are starting to understand how each living creature depends on other creatures for survival, and how the loss of even one species can affect so many others. Many people, groups, and governments have begun searching for ways to save some wild places for animals. They are working to stop the needless killing of rare animals. And they are trying to spread their message and get other people involved in the hunt for answers.

You, too, can get in on the search. A great way to start is by getting to know these rare and fascinating creatures and by learning more about their struggles for survival. Inside this book, you'll meet 22 endangered mammals, birds, and reptiles. You'll discover just how amazing they are, and how great a loss it would be if they were wiped out forever. So turn the page and join the search for ways to save creatures large and small, furry and feathered, from the fate of the dinosaurs.

Right: The giant panda is one of the most beloved animals in the world. It is also in danger of disappearing forever. Human activity has chased the panda towards extinction. Fortunately, people all over the world are working to help save the panda and other endangered animals from being wiped out.

AFRICAN ELEPHANT

With its wrinkly skin, hoselike trunk, and huge, floppy ears, the African elephant is known worldwide. What is less well known is that the African elephant, like the slightly smaller Asian elephant, is struggling to survive in the wild.

The African elephant is the largest living land mammal. It stands 12 to 13 feet high and weighs five to six tons. African elephants that live in the rain forests of central and west Africa are called forest elephants. Those that live on the plains of east and southern Africa are called savanna elephants. Elephants disappeared from the northern part of Africa centuries ago.

Some biologists believe that elephants are very intelligent and may even communicate with each other using sounds that can't be heard by human ears. There's no question that elephants are very social animals. Although the older adult males (bulls) travel alone, the younger single males may form a bachelor herd. The female elephants (cows) travel in a larger herd, accompanied by younger elephants (calves) of both sexes. The females are very protective of their young. They also share the responsibility of tending to the calves. Unlike many animals, a female elephant will adopt a calf whose mother has died. A calf weighs about 200 pounds at birth and is three feet high. It nurses for about two years. It stays with its mother, however, until it is four or five years old.

Elephants eat huge amounts of tree bark, fruits, and wild grasses. A mature five-ton elephant needs to eat about 300 pounds of vegetation daily. That's like eating 1,200 hamburgers a day! To get all the fruit and bark they need, elephants use their long tusks to uproot trees. Ironically, these tusks are the reason that elephants have been hunted for centuries. Since ancient times, the ivory tusks have been carved into objects like jewelry, piano keys, and ornaments.

Despite the laws that protect elephants in many African

Above: "Trunk-wrapping" is one way that African elephants decide who's the boss. An elephant's trunk is actually an extension of its nose and upper lip. As many as 40,000 muscles give the trunk its great strength. The two fingerlike tips on the trunk allow the elephant to pick up objects as small as a pin. **Right:** These bathing beauties show the African elephant's love of water. To quench its thirst, an elephant sucks the water up into its trunk, curls the trunk downward, and then shoots the water into its mouth and down its throat.

countries, poachers still kill the elephants for their tusks. Today, the population of elephants in Africa is under 625,000. That's less than half the size it was ten years ago. Adult male elephants are becoming extremely rare, because their large tusks make them the first target of poachers. This threatens the entire species, because the females may not be able to find mates and produce offspring. The poachers

have even begun to kill adult females and younger elephants.

Elephants are threatened not only by poaching but by the loss of their range. The growing human population in Africa has increased the demand for land that can be farmed to feed people. As humans cut trees and create farms in the elephants' range, the elephants turn to the farmers' crops for food. So the farmers view the elephants as pests.

There are a few signs, however, that the African elephant may yet be saved. In October 1989, a ban on the sale of elephant ivory was adopted by the Convention on International Trade in Endangered Species of Wild Fauna and Flora (known as CITES). Most of the 103 member nations have agreed not to allow the sale of ivory. This is an important step, because if poachers cannot sell ivory, they have no reason to kill the elephants.

Another good sign is that African nations are beginning to understand that the elephant is a major tourist attraction that can bring money into their countries. In Zimbabwe, for example, farmers who live near wildlife preserves are given a share of the proceeds earned at wildlife parks. This discourages the farmers from planting crops in the elephants' range. It also encourages the farmers to help protect the animals. In some instances, farmers are compensated for the loss of crops. This system may be adopted in Kenya, where poaching has also severely decreased the elephant population. Wildlife activists also hope to change the status of the African elephant from "threatened" to "endangered" in order to further protect this giant creature.

African elephant babies, called calves, are raised in tightly knit groups that are headed by the oldest females, called cows. Here, a cow guides her calf to food and water.

8

RHINOCEROS

The thick, platelike skin of the rhinoceros inspired the German name for this ancient creature—the Panzernashorn, or "tank rhinoceros." Sadly, the rhino is far more vulnerable than a tank. It is basically a defensive, rather than aggressive, animal. And its major defensive weapon—its horn—is useless against the bullets of poachers.

Despite more than a decade of "rhino wars" between poachers and conservationists, the rhino remains critically endangered. Over the last 25 years, the rhino population in the wild has been reduced by 85 percent. During the 1970s, the population of one species—the black rhino—dropped from 65,000 to less than 5,000.

There are five remaining rhino species. About 3,000 Asian rhinos—including the Javan, the greater one-horned, and the Sumatran—live in small reserves. The black and the white rhinos, which are both grayish-brown in color, live in Africa. Today, about 3,700 black rhinos live in 70 to 100 groups scattered throughout their former range. About 4,600 white rhinos live in wildlife reserves, and 22 live in Garamba National Park in Zaire.

All rhinos are herbivores, feeding on grasses and plants. Black rhinos are browsers, eating off of trees. Other species, such as the white rhino, are grazers, munching on plants nearer to the ground. They all share keen senses of smell and hearing, and they all have poor vision.

The smallest rhino is the Sumatran, which stands three to five feet tall. The largest is the white rhino, which stands five to six feet tall and can weigh 5,000 to nearly 8,000 pounds. All the species have at least one horn. The white, black, and Sumatran rhinos, however, each have two horns. The horns are not made of bone but of hairlike fibers, called keratin. These fibers are bonded together to form the horn, which grows on the front of the rhino's head. Although there

Above: In 1989, ten black rhinos were brought to the United States to breed in captivity. Soon after, one of those rhinos gave birth to a bouncing, 100-pound baby rhino at the Fort Worth Zoo in Texas.
Right: This big guy doesn't seem to mind a visit from a red-billed oxpecker bird. The white rhino is the largest of the rhino species. Despite their names, the white rhino and the black rhino are actually gray in color.

are differences in how rhinos compete with each other, all engage in some type of conflict. In these fights, the males use their horns to defend territory or to win a mate.

Like the elephant, killed for its valuable ivory tusks, the rhino carries a price tag on its head. But unlike ivory, the rhino's horn plays a role in the traditions of several Mideast and Asian countries. Over the centuries, the rhino horn has been thought to have medicinal power. That belief is still strong in some Asian countries, where crushed or powdered rhino horn is

used in all sorts of folk medicines. In the Mideast country of Yemen, the handles of the most prized daggers are made of rhino horn. These daggers, called jambiyya, are a national symbol of Yemen. They are traditionally given to every male when he reaches maturity. The Yemen government has banned the importation of rhino horn since 1982. Still, the government has not been able to erase this centuries-old practice.

When strict rules against killing rhinos failed to stop the slaughter, several African countries adopted shoot-to-kill policies against poachers. Even this drastic measure has not worked. In 1988, for example, five white rhinos in Kenya's Meru National Park were killed by a large group of poachers armed with machine guns. Trying to stop the poaching has simply increased the price of the rhino's horn. Today, a large rhino horn may sell for as much as $24,000. With such a price tag, it isn't hard to understand why poachers risk their own lives to kill rhinos.

Despite these obstacles, the rhino has many protectors. Since the mid-1960s, conservationists have been trying various tactics to defend the rhino. Under CITES (Convention on International Trade in Endangered Species of Wild Fauna and Flora), trade in all rhino products is banned in most countries. Rhinos have been moved to protected ranches and preserves in Africa. A small number have even been relocated to Texas.

In addition, conservationists hope to reduce the demand for rhino horn through education. They are trying to find an equally durable substitute for the rhino horn in Yemen daggers. And, they have started programs to breed rhinos in captivity. All of these efforts are aimed at giving this ancient creature a chance to survive, if only in captivity, into the 21st century.

Warriors used the black rhino's horns as symbols of power and courage for hundreds of years. They might have been surprised to discover that the rhino is a plant eater with such poor vision that it has been known to charge at bushes.

MOUNTAIN GORILLA

It wasn't until 1902 that biologists discovered the mountain gorilla in central Africa. Before that time, they believed there were only two subspecies of gorillas in Africa—the eastern lowland gorilla and the western lowland gorilla. Today, all gorillas are endangered. The mountain gorillas, however, are closest to the brink of extinction.

It is estimated that only about 400 to 450 mountain gorillas exist in the wild today. Some of them live in the Virunga Volcanoes Conservation Area, which lies on the borders of Rwanda, Zaire, and Uganda. The others live in the Bwindi Forest of southwestern Uganda.

The mountain gorilla is smaller than the eastern lowland gorilla. An adult male mountain gorilla can weigh about 440 pounds. The mountain gorilla also has shorter arms and longer hair than do the other two types of gorillas.

After the chimpanzee, the gorilla is man's closest living relative in the animal world. Although gorillas may not look much like people, they actually share some common characteristics with people.

Mountain gorillas live in small groups of between ten and 20. Each group is led by a silverback, named for the silvery hair that spreads across the back of the adult male. The silverback is the protector of the group. The other gorillas obey him. The group may also include another adult male (usually related to the silverback), several adult

Above: Baby gorillas are very playful creatures. They enjoy wrestling with each other and swinging on vines. And, much like human youngsters, they throw temper tantrums when they don't get what they want. **Right:** The adult male gorilla is called a "silverback," after the silvery hair that grows on its back.

females, and young gorillas of both sexes. When males reach adulthood (at about 15 years of age), they are forced out of the group. Usually they travel alone until they can attract females and form a group of their own. When females reach adulthood (at about ten years of age), they also usually leave their original groups. Instead of traveling alone, however,

they transfer to another group or join up with a lone male.

The members of the group travel and play together. Every night, each gorilla makes a "nest" of leaves and branches on the ground in which to sleep. During the day, the gorillas spend most of their time eating plants, leaves, tree bark, and fruit. In the early afternoons, the older gorillas rest, while the youngsters play.

Female gorillas give birth to young every three to four years, depending on whether the previous offspring survived. A newborn gorilla is tinier than a human infant. It is completely dependent on its mother for food and protection. By the time the young gorilla is six months old, it can climb trees. But it spends several years with its mother learning how to eat and socialize within the group. A gorilla in captivity can live to be about 50 years old. Most gorillas in the wild, however, are killed before they reach the age of 35.

The plight of the mountain gorilla was brought to the world's attention through a book called *Gorillas in the Mist* by Dian Fossey. Fossey spent 13 years studying gorillas in the wild. Although gorillas had been legally protected for many years, Fossey warned that they were still seriously endangered. Poachers continued to kill gorillas for their skins and hands, which were sold as souvenirs. Many gorillas also died because they got caught in traps set for other animals. Although the gorillas often were able to get out of the traps, their injuries caused infections that eventually killed them.

Today, the Mountain Gorilla Project is supported by many wildlife groups. The project was set up to continue the research on mountain gorillas. It also offers tours to people who would like to see gorillas in the wild. Small tour groups are allowed to observe the

Gorillas spend most of their days eating and sleeping in a family group, which is headed by a silverback. Here, a group of gorillas takes a break to munch on some tree bark.

gorillas for about an hour at a time. The money from the tourism is used to protect the gorillas. Some of it is also given to nearby farmers. This is done so that the local people will view the gorilla as an economic resource that needs to be protected.

The use of tourism to protect the gorilla has been questioned, however. Some people fear that too much human activity around the gorillas may be harmful to these wild creatures. No one knows how this human contact will affect the gorillas' reproduction or group activities. Some people also fear that human diseases can be transmitted to the gorillas.

On the other hand, there may be few other choices. African countries have been successful in preserving some of the gorilla's habitat and encouraging protection through such tourism. Although it may be risky, putting mountain gorillas on "exhibit" has given them another chance to survive in the wild.

Although gorillas are usually gentle, social creatures, they will attack if they feel threatened. Before attacking, though, they'll call out, tear off branches and throw them in the air, beat their chests, and pound the ground with their fists to frighten the "invader" away.

OKAPI

By the year 1900, it was thought that most large mammals in the world had been identified. That's why zoologists were very surprised when Sir Harry Johnston, a British explorer, reported the existence of an unusual and unidentified animal. His 1901 report told of a strange, short-necked "giraffe" living in the rain forests of northern Zaire in central Africa. Native Africans called this animal the okapi. Zoologists combined the natives' name for the animal with the explorer's name and called the newly discovered species Okapia johnstoni.

After some study, biologists decided that the okapi is related to the extinct ancestors of the giraffe. Giraffes are fairly common throughout Africa. They live on the savannas, or plains, of Africa. There, they use their long necks to eat leaves off the tops of trees. In contrast, okapis live only in the forested areas of north and northeastern Zaire. The okapi is

also much smaller than the giraffe. The okapi stands about five to six feet high at the shoulder. That's about as tall as a small horse. It doesn't need a long neck like a giraffe does, because the okapi eats the leaves of plants and trees that grow much closer to the forest floor. The okapi has a shiny, deep brown coat, with black-and-white stripes on its legs and hindquarters. The male of the species has short horns on its head. The horns are covered with skin except for the blunt, polished tips. Unlike many other species, the female okapi is usually larger than the male.

Researchers know very little about the life of the okapi. The first study of the okapi in the wild began only a few years ago. Biologists don't even have a good estimate of how many okapis exist in the world, because the animal is difficult to spot. Its coloring and its ability to stand perfectly still for up to an hour allow the okapi to blend into its forest habitat. In addition, the

Above: Each day, the okapi may travel more than half a mile through the thick African rain forest in search of food. In just a few days of walking and eating, it may snack on more than 100 different kinds of plants. To get a mouthful to munch, the animal wraps its long tongue around the leaves and pulls. **Right:** Adult okapis usually travel alone. The male and female of the species usually get together only to mate. Here, a female okapi stands guard over her cute calf.

okapi is usually a very quiet animal, except during mating season when it searches for a mate. All of these factors make it very difficult for people to learn much about this mysterious creature.

The okapi appears to be very solitary. It roams by itself in search of leaves to eat. Unlike many other large mammals, it does not eat fruits. Adult okapis don't appear to have natural enemies. Leopards, however, do prey on young okapis, or calves.

With its solitary lifestyle and specialized diet, the shy okapi is like the giant panda. Neither is well equipped for survival in a changing world. Unlike many large mammals, the okapi is not threatened as much by hunting as by the loss of rain forests. Under national law in Zaire, the okapi has been protected from hunters since 1933. But as the human population expands, more and more trees are cut down to make room for people. As companies use the forests for logging, coal mining, and coffee growing, the okapi's habitat shrinks.

The Zaire Institute for the Conservation of Nature has taken steps to help save the okapi. An inner region of the Ituri Forest has been designated as a national park and forest reserve. People in Zaire are also becoming very protective of the okapi. It is hoped that they will continue efforts to preserve a place for the okapi, so that this unusual animal can continue to live in the wild.

This captive okapi displays the rainbow of colors typical of the species. The okapi has a red forehead, pale yellow cheeks, a deep brown (almost purple) back, black-and-white striped hindquarters and legs, and black rings above its hooves. Its beautiful coat, along with its ability to stand completely still, helps it to hide from enemies in its native forest habitat.

TIGER

Who knows why the tiger is such a fascinating creature? Perhaps it is because of the tiger's beautiful, bold stripes. Perhaps it is because the tiger is the largest cat in the world—bigger than the lion, the so-called king of the jungle. Or perhaps it is simply that a picture of a tiger stalking its prey reminds us of a pet cat padding through the yard in pursuit of a bird. For whatever reason, many people love tigers.

Most people who love tigers, however, don't have to worry about having one in their yard. The story is different in countries such as India, where most of the remaining wild tigers live. India is crowded with people. As the human population continues to grow, there is bound to be conflict between tigers and people. Although the tigers and people who live in India can never live close together, those who want to save the tiger are trying to learn how tigers and people can share the land.

Long ago, several subspecies of tigers ranged all over Asia. Today,

three of those subspecies—the Caspian, the Javan, and the Balinese—are extinct. Another, the Chinese tiger, has all but vanished from the wild. The Sumatran, the Indo-Chinese, and the Siberian (the largest tiger) are also on the brink of extinction. The Bengal tiger, which lives in India, has been making a comeback, but it is still endangered.

For many years, tigers were hunted for sport. Indeed, at one time, a tiger-head trophy was one of the most prized possessions of the hunter. Tigers were also hunted for their skins, which were made into clothing and rugs, and for their bones, which were ground up to make folk medicines.

When some Asian countries realized that their tigers were disappearing, they passed laws to protect the animals. Russia banned the hunting of tigers about 40 years ago. China forbade tiger hunting about 30 years ago. Unfortunately, the total tiger population continued to decline.

Above: Like the much smaller cats that are kept by people as pets, these captive Bengal tigers help to groom each other's fur. In the wild, adult tigers get together only to mate. **Right:** The Siberian tiger is the largest of the tigers. The fur of this very rare cat is longer, softer, and lighter in color than the fur of tigers that live in warmer areas.

While the laws protected the tiger from hunters, they did not protect the animal from a loss of habitat. As a top predator, the tiger needs a wide range in which to hunt. It also needs plenty of prey. Although the tiger does not eat every day, it can consume between 40 and 80 pounds of meat at one meal. It usually hunts large mammals, such as moose and deer, by following the animals and preying on the weak or young. Unlike lions, which live and hunt in groups all year long, tigers only live in pairs for a brief time when the cubs are born. Most of the time, tigers hunt alone.

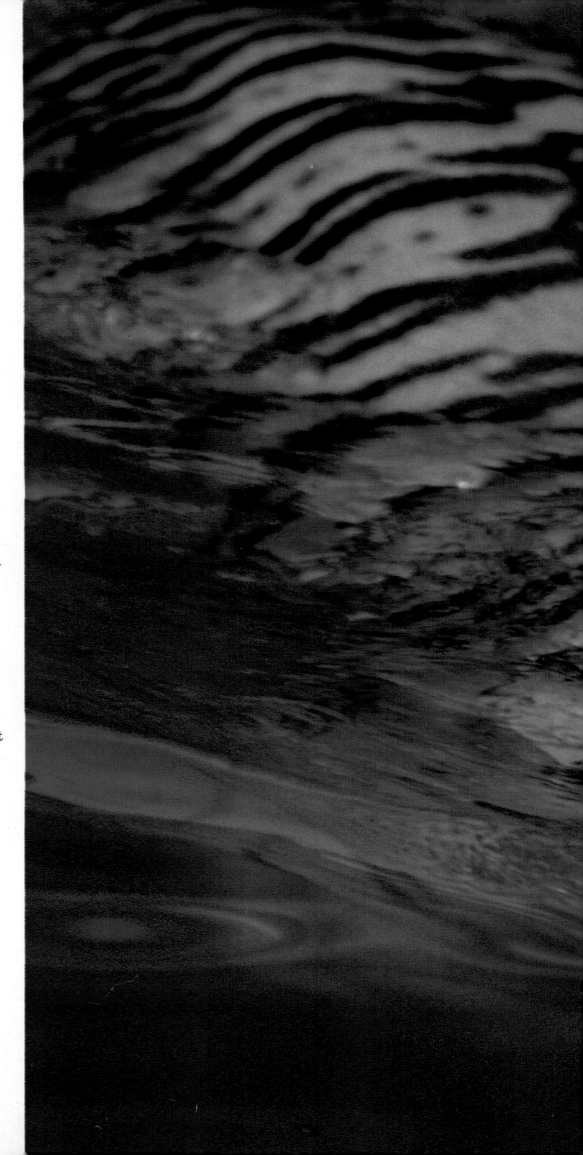

As the human population continued to expand in countries such as India, and as land was cleared for ranches and farms, the tigers were forced deeper into the forests to find prey. Eventually, the tigers couldn't find enough wild prey, so they began stalking the cattle. Sometimes, an old or weak tiger that couldn't hunt very well killed people. These confrontations between man and tiger usually ended in the death of the tiger.

By 1972, the Bengal tiger population in India had dropped alarmingly low. Within the span of 50 years, the largest tiger population in the world had fallen from 42,000 to less than 2,000. It became clear that if such decline continued, the Bengal tiger and other Asian tigers would soon be extinct.

In 1973, the World Wildlife Fund began an international campaign called Operation Tiger. This program raised money to establish reserves for tigers all over Asia. As part of this effort, India established six tiger reserves. Villages were moved out of the reserves. This not only gave the tiger more room to roam, it also allowed the tiger's prey to repopulate the area. As a result of this successful campaign, the Bengal tiger population today numbers more than 4,000.

Efforts to save the tiger are continuing. Although tigers are breeding very well in captivity, it is very difficult to put captive tigers into the wild. So, conservationists are concentrating their efforts on preserving a place for the tigers that are in the wild. The reserves have brightened the outlook for the tiger. But the struggle to find ways for a growing human population to share scarce land with the tiger is by no means complete.

Unlike many other cats, the tiger is a good swimmer. It appears to enjoy bathing and will often lie around in shallow water to keep itself cool on a hot day.

CHEETAH

The cheetah is the fastest animal on land. It has been estimated that, in very short sprints, the cheetah can reach a speed of between 50 and 60 miles per hour. The cheetah, like tigers and other cats, stalks its prey. It creeps up on its unsuspecting victim and then pounces. But unlike other cats, it can also chase its prey for a short time. As it runs, the cheetah keeps its head motionless so that it can keep its prey in sight. Although the cheetah is much smaller than the lion and the tiger, its speed and skill allow it to successfully hunt for food on the open plains.

Along with this sprinting ability, there are other reasons why cheetahs are considered to be very specialized cats. The cheetah is the only large cat that can't fully retract, or pull in, its claws. Because its legs are very straight, the cheetah cannot climb trees like other cats. The only way it can get up into a tree is by running up a

limb that is hanging close to the ground. And, unlike other large cats, the cheetah has a flexible spine that increases its swiftness.

The cheetah measures about six feet long, including its two-foot-long tail. It weighs about 90 to 140 pounds. Its fur is light brown or light gray with black spots. It has black rings on its tail. It also has a patch of black in the shape of a teardrop under each eye.

The cheetah once ranged over most of Africa, Arabia, the Middle East, and northern India. The ancient Egyptians even kept cheetahs as pets. Today, the cheetah has disappeared from Asia and northern Africa. It is found only in sections of Africa south of the Sahara desert. There are probably only between 5,000 and 15,000 cheetahs in the world.

The cheetah hunts gazelles and impalas in the open African plains, called the savanna. Both lions and cheetahs live on the savanna, but

Above: The female cheetah has a litter of two to four kittens at a time. The kittens stay with their mother until they are able to hunt for themselves. **Right:** Cheetah kittens sport coats of long, blue-gray hair with dark spots. After about three months, the hair is replaced by fur that is sandy brown in color and marked by dark spots.

unlike lions, cheetahs do not live in groups. Sometimes they hunt in pairs, and sometimes young males will stay together for a while. But the cheetah is mostly a loner. The cheetah needs a large range in which to hunt its prey.

Like many African animals, cheetahs are being run out of their natural habitat. More and more people are moving into traditional cheetah territory. As they do so, less land is available for cheetahs and their prey. Cheetahs are protected in most countries. But sometimes the laws are ignored, and cheetahs

are shot as pests because they kill small farm animals for food. Conservationists are hoping to move these "problem" cheetahs into wildlife preserves in other countries in an attempt to save the cheetah from extinction.

Unlike lions and tigers, most zoos have found it very difficult to breed cheetahs. At the Cincinnati Zoo, for example, keepers have discovered that cheetahs don't react well to the food that suits most cats. Now the zoo is feeding the cheetahs a different diet to see if that improves the cats' ability to reproduce.

In addition, all the remaining cheetahs in the world appear to be very closely related genetically. This poses another threat to the cheetah's survival, because it increases the chance that genetic defects will develop and wipe out the population.

Most animals that develop a highly specialized diet or habitat are very vulnerable to extinction. Even a slight change in the way they live can threaten the species. This is certainly true of the cheetah, the most specialized wild cat in the world. But the struggle to find a wild place for the cheetah in today's changing world continues.

Over short distances, the cheetah can run faster than any other land animal. Its heavy tail provides balance and allows the cheetah to make sudden, sharp turns.

JAGUAR

When most people think of large wild cats, they think of lions and tigers, or perhaps even leopards. Most people don't know that the jaguar is the largest cat in North and South America. It is between eight and nine feet long, including its three-foot long tail. It can weigh up to 300 pounds.

The jaguar prefers to live in dense, forested areas in tropical climates, where it can prowl through trees looking for prey. The jaguar also is a good swimmer and likes to live near water. Like tigers, jaguars hunt alone and have their own territories. Male and female jaguars only get together to mate. Every other year, females have a litter of two to four cubs.

The jaguar once roamed as far north as Texas and New Mexico. Today, the jaguar can be found only in remote areas of Central and South America. The jaguar populations in El Salvador, Uruguay, and Chile have probably

already been wiped out. The cats face the same fate in Argentina, Costa Rica, and Panama. The jaguar is considered endangered throughout its range even in areas of Central and South America that are not heavily populated with people.

Like the other spotted or striped cats, jaguars were hunted for their beautiful skins. The creamy yellow fur has patterns of black circles with black spots in the center. It was the demand for this fur that wiped out the jaguars in most populated areas. Trade in jaguar skins has been banned for many years. Laws protecting the jaguar, however, are not very well enforced. The jaguar is still hunted for sport. But most of the killing today occurs because jaguars prey on farm animals.

Unlike many large cats, the jaguar is considered an "opportunistic" feeder. This means that the jaguar is less fussy about

Above: The jaguar usually has creamy yellow or orange fur, with black spots on its head and legs. Its back and sides are marked by patterns of black circles around black spots. In some rare cases, the jaguar may be born with whitish fur or nearly black fur. **Right:** Breeding times of the jaguar vary. The mother gives birth to up to four spotted cubs at a time. She has the sole responsibility of raising the young, who stay with her for about two years.

what it eats than many other large mammals. Usually it eats small mammals, but it also likes to feed on turtles. It simply waits by a river for the turtle to crawl out of the water. The jaguar will also feed on cattle and dogs, which is the main reason it is still killed by farmers today. Although every country in the animal's range has laws to protect jaguars, most of the South American countries permit the

killing of wild animals for the protection of farm animals.

It's very likely that the main reason jaguars still exist is that, until recently, their jungle homes weren't much in demand by people. But as the human population in South America grows, more and more jungle area is cleared by loggers, and more and more land is farmed. Ranchers and farmers view the jaguar as a pest, in much the same way that ranchers and farmers in the United States view the Western coyote. Ranchers and farmers don't see any benefit in protecting animals that steal their food and perhaps even threaten their children.

Changing this situation is not easy. The human population in South America is growing very quickly. The people require more and more land on which to survive. So, it seems likely that the jaguar habitat will shrink.

In the long run, the only way to protect the jaguar is to involve the people who share its habitat. Indeed, such efforts have already begun. The first jaguar preserve, called the Cockscomb Jaguar Preserve, was established in Belize, South America. The specific purpose of this preserve is to protect the jaguar, but it has also become a tourist attraction. Jaguars are also doing well in the Manu National Park, a 5,000-square-mile park in the Peruvian Amazon Basin.

It has also been suggested that governments legalize sport hunting of jaguars in an attempt to regulate the killing. Money earned from licenses or permits could be shared with local people. The nearby residents would then have a reason to help protect the jaguar. By killing some jaguars legally, governments might be able to help protect the majority of jaguars living in the wild.

The jaguar will often hide in trees or bushes to surprise its prey. It prefers deer, birds, tapirs, and fish, but it will also eat dogs, monkeys, sheep, cattle, and horses.

SNOW LEOPARD

For centuries, the snow leopard was hunted for its fur. Its smoky-gray fur, accented with black spots, is one of the most beautiful in the world. It is also very hard to come by, because the snow leopard has always been very rare and elusive. The snow leopard's continued, though endangered, existence is probably due only to the fact that it lives in some of the most remote areas of the world.

The snow leopard lives only in very high mountainous areas in central Asia. Long ago, it adapted to the snow-covered Himalayan Mountains by becoming one of the world's best mountain climbers. The snow leopard's chest is extremely well-developed, giving it the power to withstand high altitudes and the ability to leap across rocky crevices. It has huge, heavily padded forepaws that allow it to get a good grip on steep cliffs. Its long tail

provides balance as it prowls narrow mountain pathways. And its fur provides camouflage against the snow and rocks, so that the snow leopard can stalk its prey.

No one knows how many snow leopards exist today, because these animals are so difficult to track. It is believed that they still inhabit the mountains of Afghanistan, Bhutan, China, India, Mongolia, Nepal, Pakistan, and the Soviet Union. But they are very rare in each of these countries. They may even be extinct in some of them.

Snow leopards are related to most other large cats. They are solitary hunters. They prey on wild sheep, goats, and other mammals. The snow leopard mates in early spring. The baby leopards, or cubs, are born in June. By the age of two, the cubs can hunt on their own.

A recent study of snow leopards in Nepal suggests that snow leopards

Above: During the winter, snow leopards usually spend their time in lower mountain elevations, where it is warmer. In the summer, the cats may climb to heights of 18,000 feet. **Right:** Because the snow leopard's habitat cuts across several Asian countries, efforts to save this cat require cooperation among these nations.

are different from other African and Asian cats in their unusual "sharing" of territory. Like other large cats, snow leopards make scratching marks and spray their urine to mark their territory. But the territories of most other large male cats overlap only with female cats. Even female cats usually have their own territories. Young tigers, for example, quickly learn not to move into another tiger's territory, because they could be killed. Snow

leopards are unusual because their territories overlap. They cross over each other's territories but are seldom seen together. This may be because snow leopards must use the same narrow paths to cross mountains.

Under international agreements, the trading of snow leopard skins has been forbidden for many years. But even these agreements can't guarantee the survival of the snow leopard in today's changing world. Like other predators at the top of the food chain, the snow leopard needs a large hunting range and enough prey to survive. As people push farther into remote areas in order to graze their sheep and goats, the wild range of the snow leopard shrinks. Unable to find wild prey, the hungry snow leopards feed on the grazing sheep.

In Nepal, a mountainous country that separates Tibet from India, the government is creating special areas for wild animals. To prevent people from using the land to graze sheep, it is giving the money earned from tourism to the nearby residents. This encourages people to support the national conservation areas. It also gives them a reason to protect the snow leopards. Conservationists are hoping that other countries will establish similar havens in the Himalayas. Without such cooperation, a snow leopard saved in one country could easily die when it crosses into another. After all, snow leopards, like all animals, don't pay attention to borders drawn on maps.

The snow leopard's soft fur is made up of two layers. The thick undercoat traps warm air next to the cat's body. The bulky outer coat provides a shield against icy winds.

BLACK-FOOTED FERRET

Unlike some of the mammals facing extinction, the black-footed ferret doesn't inspire huge, well-funded protection campaigns. Luckily, there are a few ferret fans who are working hard to save this very rare mammal.

The black-footed ferret is related to weasels, mink, and badgers. They all belong to the mammal group called mustelids. The black-footed ferret is usually 18 to 20 inches long, including its five-inch tail. It weighs between one and a half and two and a half pounds. It is brownish in color, with a dark mask around its eyes, dark feet, and a dark tip on its tail. The black-footed ferret should not be confused with the fitch ferret, which is domesticated and plentiful. The fitch ferret is sold in pet stores. The black-footed ferret, which may no longer exist in the wild, is totally protected as an endangered species.

Humans are not *directly* responsible for the disappearance of the black-footed ferret. That does not mean, however, that humans

did not play a role. The tragedy of the ferret illustrates the way many animals depend on each other for food. It also shows how man's interference can cause ripples throughout the plant and animal worlds.

Ferrets and prairie dogs lived together in the Great Plains for thousands of years. At one time, there may have been more than a million ferrets spread out over 12 western states and two Canadian provinces.

Long ago, the ferret became almost entirely dependent on the prairie dog for food. The ferret also used the prairie dog's burrow for shelter. When ranchers and farmers moved into the plains, they nearly wiped out the prairie dogs. The ranchers saw the prairie dogs as pests, because they ate the grass used to feed cattle. The farmers wanted to clear the land in order to plant crops. So, to eliminate the prairie dog colonies, poisoned grain was spread over millions of acres of land. Some ferrets died when they

Above: Cautious and alert, the black-footed ferret peaks out of the prairie-dog burrow in which it lives. The masked creature emerges from its home only under the cover of darkness to hunt for food, search for new burrows, and find a mate.
Right: This black-footed ferret is doing what researchers call "periscoping." With only its head and upper shoulders above the ground, the ferret turns in a complete circle to survey the area around its home.

ate the poisoned prairie dogs. Many more died because they could no longer find enough food.

By the 1950s, there were so few black-footed ferrets that many people thought they were extinct. Then, in 1964, a small group of ferrets was discovered on a South Dakota ranch. By studying this group, researchers discovered that ferrets are solitary creatures that hunt and feed at night, making them hard to spot. Also, ferrets live underground in prairie-dog burrows, which makes them even more difficult to find.

When the group of ferrets in South Dakota disappeared, it wasn't until 1981 that black-footed ferrets were found again. This time, researchers counted 129 ferrets at the base of the Carter Mountains in Wyoming. Because of the small number, it was recommended that a few ferrets be captured. These captive ferrets would form a breeding colony. So, in 1985, six young black-footed ferrets were captured.

The number of wild ferrets continued to decline, however, following a plague among prairie dogs. In addition, one of the captive ferrets died. So researchers captured six more ferrets. And it was a good thing they did, because the remaining ferrets in the original captive group died.

Using the surviving captive ferrets, a successful captive-breeding program was set up by the Wyoming Game and Fish Department. Today, the captive ferret population in Wyoming is doing well. The program managers, however, hope to introduce black-footed ferrets that are not related to those already in captivity. Bringing in new blood could increase the ferret's chances of surviving. In 1989, Wildlife Conservation International began offering a $5,000 reward to anyone who finds a wild black-footed ferret. Several organizations and government agencies are cooperating in the project to give the black-footed ferret another chance for survival.

The male black-footed ferret is called a hob; the female, a gill. The gill gives birth to a litter of one to five babies, or kits, in May and June. The kits spend their first month close to their mother. During that time, the mother may move her young from burrow to burrow to ensure their safety.

KEY DEER

Long ago when the Ice Age ended, the glaciers melted. This raised sea levels around the world. Much of the coastal areas became covered with water, creating many islands. Some of the animals that existed at that time found themselves "caught" on these islands. They were separated by miles of ocean from the rest of their species on the mainland. In the thousands of years that followed, many of these animals adapted to their island homes. These adaptations made them different from their relatives on the mainland. The Key deer, which is considered a subspecies of the white-tailed deer, is one such "island" animal.

Key deer live only on a string of small islands off the tip of Florida. These islands are called the Florida Keys. Because they have adapted to their island home, the Key deer are now quite distinct from the white-tailed deer that live all over the Florida mainland.

First of all, Key deer look like miniature deer. They are only about two feet high at the shoulder—much shorter than white-tailed deer. Key deer are also different because the female, or doe, only has one baby, or fawn. The white-tailed doe, on the other hand, usually gives birth to two fawns after each mating. Yet, in other ways, Key deer are similar to white-tailed deer. They both tend to live in small groups. Both also eat a wide variety of plants.

Key deer were discovered by European explorers. It wasn't until about 40 years ago, however, that people began to realize that hunters had nearly wiped out the Key deer. To protect the remaining deer, the National Key Deer Wildlife Refuge was created in 1954. But, despite

Above: Like other male deer, Key deer bucks have antlers. The antlers are shed once a year and replaced by new ones. Here, two Key deer bucks engage in combat to win females. **Right:** The pale-coated Key deer is much smaller than its white-tailed cousins on the mainland. It stands only about two feet high at the shoulder.

this protection, the population continued to decline. Some Key deer were killed by poachers, who ignored the laws protecting the animals. Many more were killed accidentally by cars. Some were even killed by dogs. By the late 1970s, the population of Key deer was only about 400 animals.

Today, the Key deer population is between 250 and 300. Naturalists at the refuge believe that the population is stable. Unfortunately, it doesn't appear to be growing.

Traffic accidents and loss of wilderness continue to threaten the Key deer.

The National Key Deer Refuge includes about 7,400 acres. About 2,000 acres are on Big Pine Key. The rest of the refuge is spread out over more than 24 smaller outlying islands. Key deer live in all these areas. During drought seasons, however, most of the Key deer swim to Big Pine Key for fresh water. When the refuge was first established, it was surrounded by wilderness. But as more and more land is developed for homes and stores, the deer lose more and more of their habitat.

Development also brings more people and more traffic. There is only one major road that goes from the mainland of Florida to Key West, the city at the farthest end of the Keys. That same road, U.S. 1, also goes right through the deer refuge. As local and tourist traffic increases, more and more deer are killed when they cross roads.

Naturalists at the refuge are trying to lower these traffic deaths by strictly enforcing speed laws. They are also trying to clear the roadsides to improve visibility, so that drivers can avoid deer on the road. Naturalists also warn people not to feed the deer. Although people may have good intentions, feeding the deer can actually hurt them. When they're fed by people, the deer are attracted to populated areas, which increases their chances of being hit by cars.

The female Key deer, unlike the white-tailed doe, has only one fawn after each mating. Like many other baby deer, however, the Key deer fawn sports pretty white spots.

46

WOODLAND CARIBOU

Although you may not be familiar with the word caribou, chances are you've heard fanciful stories and songs about these creatures. Caribou, especially those that are raised in captivity, are better known as reindeer. There are two kinds of North American caribou. Woodland caribou tend to live in the forested areas of the far north in Alaska, Canada, and Greenland. Barren ground caribou live even farther north on the frozen, treeless Arctic plains, known as tundra.

Caribou stand between four and five feet high at the shoulder. A male caribou can weigh 700 pounds although most caribou weigh about 500 pounds. The caribou's brownish-gray fur, which provides good protection in the winter, is shed in the spring. Unlike most members of the deer family, the females, as well as the males, have antlers. The males shed their antlers in late fall. The females shed their antlers in the spring.

Like many other members of the deer family, caribou travel in herds. Woodland caribou usually travel in herds of 50, whereas barren ground caribou have been known to travel in herds of as many as 80,000 to 100,000. The herds migrate regularly to find food and to mate. They stay in more southern wooded areas in the winter and move north in the spring.

With its large, hoofed feet, the caribou is well equipped to handle muddy ground in the spring and frozen ground in the winter. In the fall, the caribou grows a horny edge around the outside of each hoof, which allows it to get a better grip on the ice in the winter.

Like other kinds of deer, the caribou is a "cud chewer." Instead of having front teeth in the roof of its mouth, the caribou has a hard plate of bone, which it uses to tear off food. The caribou swallows the food whole. The swallowed food goes to one part of the caribou's four-part

Above: Woodland caribou breed in the fall. One or two young are born about seven and a half months later. Like all reindeer, woodland caribou are strong swimmers. **Right:** In winter, caribou feed on a type of moss, called lichen, which they uncover from beneath the snow with their feet. In summer, they eat grasses and saplings.

stomach. When the animal rests, it brings the swallowed food—now called cud—back up into its mouth and grinds it up. The woodland caribou likes to eat a special kind of moss, called lichen, although it will also eat twigs and grasses.

During mating season, each male gathers a group of females and fights off other males using its antlers. Baby caribou are born in June. They weigh about nine pounds and are able to run within a half hour after birth, so that they can keep up with the herd.

The main predator of the caribou is the wolf. Packs of wolves follow caribou herds and prey on weak or injured animals. Wolves, however, are not responsible for the threatened existence of the caribou. For centuries, people have hunted the caribou. The Inuits (Eskimos) of Alaska and Canada relied on the caribou for food and clothing, much like American Indians relied on the buffalo. But sport hunters killed off far more caribou.

Today, woodland caribou have almost disappeared from their southern ranges. Poaching is still a problem, but it is not the only one that threatens the survival of the wild reindeer. Logging in the northern woodlands continues to decrease the amount of forested area available to the caribou. In addition, the construction of oil pipelines may affect the woodland caribou's usual migration from the north to the southern wooded areas. The pipelines appear to frighten the female caribou that are nursing their young. Although this human activity does not appear to disturb the male caribou, it may interfere with caribou reproduction or with the unity of the caribou herds. Additional research may tell us more about how human activity affects the woodland caribou. Hopefully, it will also show us ways to help save the woodland caribou from being wiped out in North America.

Antlers vary in size and shape from caribou to caribou. Even on the same caribou, one antler may be different from the other. The male's antlers, which can grow to a length of four feet, are usually larger than those of the female.

TIMBER WOLF

As soon as colonists reached the shores of North America, they began killing the timber wolf. Before the American Revolution, hunters were paid bounties for the bodies of dead wolves. In this century, a federal poisoning program almost eliminated the wolf from the lower 48 states. In Yellowstone National Park, wolf packs had vanished by the 1930s.

Today, the entire North American wolf population numbers only about 40,000. Most of these wolves live in Alaska and Canada. About 1,200 live in northern Minnesota. There are also a few other scattered populations in northern Michigan and in the northern Rocky Mountains. The wolves in Minnesota are considered threatened. Those living in the other lower 48 states are considered endangered and are protected today. Their future, however, is by no

means secure. There is strong opposition to plans for reintroducing wolves into Yellowstone and parts of the northern Rocky Mountains.

The timber wolf is also called the gray wolf and the lobo. A wolf's color can vary from dirty white to black, but the fur of most wolves is gray. Wolves are unusual because they appear to mate for life. By the time a female wolf is two years old, she can reproduce. A litter consists of from two to 13 pups.

Adult wolves weigh between 60 and 130 pounds—enough to overpower a small deer. They make the most of their hunting ability, however, by hunting in packs. A pack can consist of up to 20 wolves. The young wolves and a few older adults wait while most of the pack hunts herds of deer, elk, caribou, or moose. The pack will chase a herd, looking for a weak or young animal. Then, the wolves work together to

Above: Timber wolves hunt at night. They may cover as many as 50 miles in search of prey. While they usually prey on elk, moose, deer, and caribou, they may also attack sheep and cattle. **Right:** Despite its shyness around humans and its resemblance to "man's best friend," the timber wolf has been feared, hated, and hunted for hundreds of years.

separate their prey from the herd. Like lions, wolves have strict rules about eating. The leader of the pack eats first, then the other males, then the females, then the youngsters. If wolves do not have enough prey, the youngsters quickly die.

Although wolves are very difficult to spot in the wild, people can usually identify the wolf's howl. Indeed, the howl is probably the wolf's best-known characteristic. No one knows for sure why wolves howl. It may have something to do

with the fact that each wolf pack
has its own territory. The howl may
be the pack's way of warning other
wolves to stay off their turf.

Unlike many animals facing
extinction, the wolf's endangered
status is not caused by loss of
habitat or prey. Wolves are
endangered strictly because people
don't want them around. In the
wild, wolves are very shy of
humans. But like many predators,
wolves will feed on cattle and sheep.
This is why ranchers living in
Montana and around Yellowstone
National Park object to the United
States Fish and Wildlife Service
plans to reintroduce the wolf into
these areas. Hunters also are
opposed to this plan, because they
view wolves as competitors in the
hunt for deer and elk. The Wildlife
Service, however, believes that
wolves could help control the
growing elk populations.

Those in favor of the plan point to
Minnesota. It is there that most of
the wolves in the continental United
States live. The Minnesota wolves
live around farms, but they kill few
of the livestock. If a cow or sheep is
killed, the farmer is compensated.
In the recovery plan for the
northern Rocky Mountains, the
wolf-control program would deal
with problem wolves, provide
compensation for ranchers who lose
livestock, and manage other
problems that might arise.

Proving that wolf packs can
coexist with people, however, is no
easy task. Even in Minnesota, the
wolf is not universally accepted. In a
single week during 1989, four
wolves in a study group of 33 were
found shot. One of them was a
female wolf that had been tagged
and followed for eight years.
Unfortunately, the Endangered
Species Act couldn't protect her
from the fate of many of her
ancestors—death at the hands of a
human hunter.

Timber wolves appear to mate for life. The
female gives birth to a litter of four to
fourteen pups at a time. All the family
members share in the care of the pups.

GIANT PANDA

Scientists have long argued about whether the giant panda is more closely related to the bear or to the racoon. It walks like a bear. And recent studies have shown that its blood and genetic structure relate it to the bear. But the giant panda doesn't hibernate, as most bears do. In addition, its teeth are more like the teeth of the red panda, a member of the racoon family. In the 1800s, scientists tried to solve this problem by giving the giant panda its own genus, or category, called Ailuropoda. Still, the debate continues. What no one argues about is that the giant panda is one of the best-known and most-loved animals in the world. The affection for the panda, as well as the fact that it is endangered, have made it an international symbol of wildlife preservation.

At one time, giant pandas roamed throughout China. Today, it is estimated that about 1,000 giant pandas exist in the wild. That number appears to be declining every year, despite legal protection,

panda reserves, harsh penalties for killing pandas, and a well-funded conservation program. Fewer than 100 pandas live in captivity, most of them in China. Those living in the wild are in the far west mountainous area of China. Their range covers only about 11,000 square miles in three Chinese provinces. There, China has established 12 panda reserves.

The giant panda's future appears to depend on efforts to solve at least three problems. The first problem centers around the panda's habitat. The giant panda spends its waking hours searching for and eating large amounts of bamboo. It relies almost solely on about 20 varieties of bamboo for food. Bamboo is a type of grass that flowers and dies every 20 to 120 years, depending on the variety. When one variety of bamboo dies, every bamboo plant of that kind dies at about the same time.

As the human population expands, more and more of the panda's habitat is cleared. This expansion has left "islands" of

Above: The People's Republic of China used the popular giant panda as a symbol of friendship when it renewed relations with Western countries in the 1970s.
Right: Bamboo is the giant panda's main source of food. The panda has a special thumblike bone on each of its front paws that helps it to get a sturdy grip on bamboo stalks.

bamboo. The pandas living in these isolated patches have been cut off from each other and from other sources of bamboo. When one variety of bamboo dies off, the pandas die if they cannot find other kinds of bamboo to eat. Unlike some other species, the panda does not appear to be able to adapt its diet to the loss of bamboo. It is unable to substitute other foods. So, in order to save this creature, efforts are needed to increase, or at least maintain, the panda's habitat.

A second major problem that must be overcome is poaching. China has severe penalties for killing pandas.

In addition, almost every country forbids the sale of panda skins. Still, poaching continues to threaten the panda's survival. To add to the problem, some pandas are killed accidentally when they get caught in traps set for other animals.

The third problem is the panda's poor breeding record in captivity. Newborn pandas are only a few inches long at birth. They are also totally dependent on their mothers for their first year and a half of life. Until recently, most breeding programs outside of China failed to produce offspring that could survive. At the National Zoo in Washington, D.C., biologists have been disappointed several times by the deaths of offspring of Ling-Ling and Hsing-Hsing. These two famous pandas were given to the United States government by the People's Republic of China in 1972. The Chapultepec Zoo in Mexico City, however, has had some success. A giant panda couple at the zoo has produced four surviving young.

The Chinese, who have more captive pandas to work with, appear to have better success with breeding pandas in captivity. This is why many conservationists have opposed the Chinese program of briefly lending pandas to zoos around the world. Many conservationists believe the pandas should stay in China to breed in captivity. Conservationists also would like to see China reintroduce more pandas into the wild. In addition, the Chinese have been urged to set up "bamboo corridors," which would help connect isolated panda populations in the wild.

Many groups are contributing to the international effort to save the panda. It remains to be seen whether this symbol of wildlife protection can continue to survive in the wild.

Giant pandas are usually silent creatures. But infants can squawk, and adults have the ability to make several sounds, including honks, barks, chirps, growls, · and roars.

GRIZZLY BEAR

Native Americans called the grizzly "the beast that walks like man." Not knowing about the apes in Africa, many tribes thought of the grizzly as man's closest relative. The bear's ability to stand on its hind legs wasn't the only reason.

The Native Americans recognized that the grizzly is different from most animals. The mother bears are very protective of their young. They carefully teach their cubs how and where to hunt. The grizzly also seems to have an amazing memory. It can return year after year to the best berry patches. And it is skilled and patient enough to catch fish with its huge paws.

The sight of these giant beasts stunned the European explorers who came to North America. This bear was much bigger than the European brown bear. The explorers named the grizzly after its gray-tipped, or "grizzled," fur. What the explorers didn't know was that the grizzly is very closely related to the European brown bear. In fact, some biologists believe the two are

actually the same kind of bear. They just happen to live in different places. The grizzly bear is also very closely related to the Alaskan brown bear.

When it stands on all fours, the grizzly measures about four to five feet high at the shoulder and about six and a half to nine feet long. Adult males continue to grow throughout their lives. They can weigh more than 900 pounds. To maintain this huge size, grizzlies are "opportunistic" feeders. Most animals are either "carnivores" (meat eaters) or "herbivores" (plant eaters). Grizzly bears, however, are "omnivores." They eat meat when they can get it, but they can also survive on a diet of plants. Their flexible feeding habits allow them to adapt to a variety of settings, including mountains, plains, and forests.

Cold weather doesn't bother the grizzly either. Like most bears, grizzlies hibernate in winter. They dig a den in November and sleep until spring. During hibernation,

Above: After a successful fishing trip in an icy river, a grizzly bear carries its catch of salmon to the river bank to dine. While grizzlies enjoy meat and fish, they can also survive on plants. **Right:** For the most part, grizzly bears avoid people. Yet their huge size and fierce looks made them favorite targets of hunters for years.

they live off body fat. To store enough fat for the winter, they must eat constantly from spring to November.

In early spring, the hungry bear comes out of its den. It searches for the frozen bodies of deer or elk that didn't survive the winter. It also kills weak or young animals. In the summer, the grizzly turns to plants and berries for food. It covers a wide range in its search for plants. But it is always on the lookout for meat. A squirrel that gets too close to a berry patch can quickly become a meal.

Grizzly bears mate in May or June. This is the only time males and females spend together. The

female usually gives birth to two cubs between January and March. At birth, cubs are only about eight inches long and weigh under two pounds. They nurse until spring. The mother spends the next two or three years teaching her cubs where to build a den, how to hunt, and which plants to eat. Once the cubs have learned their lessons, she forces them to find their own territories.

Grizzlies had no enemies—until people were armed with rifles. Perhaps as many as 100,000 grizzlies once lived in the western United States. By 1900, however, they had disappeared from all but a handful of western states. Today, only very small populations of grizzlies remain. They live in or near national parks and forests in Montana, Idaho, Washington, and Wyoming. Despite receiving "threatened species" status in 1975, the grizzly population has continued to decline.

Grizzly bears generally avoid humans, but they love human garbage, which brings them into close contact with people. This is dangerous for bears because a bear that attacks a human is destroyed. Problem bears that grow too fond of feeding at dumps are relocated. They are moved in the hope that they will stay away from the dumps. This, however, also puts the bears in jeopardy, because they may have become so dependent on garbage that they starve without it.

Throughout the 1970s, Yellowstone Park officials were criticized because many bears were being destroyed. In 1983, the Interagency Grizzly Bear Committee was set up to coordinate a program to help the grizzly. This group is trying to learn how to manage the grizzly population. Given the grizzly's amazing ability to adapt, what is most needed is public support to give the grizzly a home in the wild.

Two baby grizzlies, or cubs, snuggle up to their mother for a nap. The female grizzly, or sow, gives birth to two cubs—often twins—during the winter while she is in the den.

POLAR BEAR

Stalking its prey across the frozen Arctic tundra, the polar bear seems well adapted to its harsh habitat. It's a very large creature, weighing as much as 1,400 pounds and reaching a length of up to 11 feet. But despite its huge size, the polar bear's white fur makes it almost invisible against the whiteness of the far North. The bear has little trouble creeping up on an unsuspecting seal. Nor does it have trouble staying warm as it darts through the icy Arctic sea in search of food. A layer of blubber covered by thick fur protects it from temperatures that few other mammals can endure.

The polar bear is closely related to the brown bear, which lives on land and feeds on vegetation. But the polar bear is considered a marine mammal, because it spends so much time in or near the sea. It is also one of the world's largest carnivores, or "meat eaters." Carnivores are considered the "top predators" because they are at the top of the food chain. They have no natural

enemies, other than humans. But this does not mean that there are no threats to the survival of the species. Polar bears need a large range in which to hunt. They also reproduce slowly. In addition, for many years, people have hunted the polar bear for food, fur, and sport.

The polar bear usually stays close to the shore in the winter and ventures further inland in the summer. Males seek out females during the mating season between April and June. In December, the female gives birth to one or two cubs in a small chamber that she has dug in the snow. This is known as denning. In late March or early April, the mother and cubs move out of the den. The mother stays with her cubs for about two years. She teaches them how to hunt seals and protects them until they are skilled enough to live on their own.

Wild polar bears can be found in five countries—the United States, the Soviet Union, Canada, Norway, and Greenland. The Soviet Union banned the hunting of polar bears

Above: Despite the polar bear's huge size—an adult male may be nearly 11 feet long and weigh 1,400 pounds—it is usually shy around humans. But if the bear feels threatened, it will attack. **Right:** Even in captivity, the female polar bear is very protective of her young. Here, five-month-old Frosty gets a hug from mother, Russia.

in 1956. It took the other countries much longer to begin protecting the polar bear. The United States Marine Mammal Protection Act of 1972 prohibited the use of aircraft to hunt polar bears in Alaska. In both Alaska and Canada, however, native Inuits (Eskimos) are allowed to hunt and kill polar bears for food and fur, as they have done for hundreds of years. Debate continues in both the United States and Canada about allowing this practice to continue. But both governments apparently believe that fewer bears are killed in regulated hunts than might be killed by poachers.

Conservationists see two other major threats to the survival of the polar bear—oil spills and shrinking habitat. The nearly 11 million gallons of oil spilled into Alaska's Prince William Sound in 1989 caused the immediate deaths of many animals. Biologists fear the polar bears might eat the polluted meat of dead or dying animals. They also worry that a sharp decrease in the food supply will further threaten the bears. In a fragile environment like Alaska's, even minor changes in the food chain can have drastic results. The estimated 20,000 to 25,000 polar bears left in the world are very vulnerable to such change.

The tanker spill also focused attention on Alaska's Arctic National Wildlife Refuge, which is home to many polar bears. The inland portion of this area is protected from oil exploration. The coastal plain, where much of the wildlife lives, is not. Oil exploration along the coast would disturb the bear's habitat. Since the polar bear needs a wide range in which to live, this loss of habitat would make it more difficult for the polar bear to survive in the wild. Plans by oil companies to explore and develop the coastal plain were temporarily halted by public outcry over the spill. It remains to be seen whether the human demand for resources will outweigh the needs of the polar bear and other wildlife in the Arctic.

These two young, male polar bears test their skills in a playful battle. Polar bears are strong enough to knock out a seal with a single blow and then lift their prey with one arm.

SEA OTTER

The deaths of hundreds of sea otters were among the tragic results of the 1989 oil spill off the coast of Alaska. Once thought to be nearly extinct, sea otters had finally begun to reestablish themselves in the wild. This was especially true in the area of Prince William Sound, where the spill occurred. Conservationists won't know the full extent of the damage to the sea otter population for some time. They do know, however, that this marine mammal is very vulnerable to polluted waters.

Unlike other northern marine mammals, which rely on blubber for protection from the cold, the sea otter's fur is its only insulation. Oil can quickly soil the fur, allowing cold water to reach the skin. When this happens, the otter freezes to death. This thick fur is also the reason that the sea otter was hunted nearly to extinction.

In the 18th century, sea otters lived throughout much of the Pacific coastline. Their range extended from the coast of Mexico to northern Alaska and Japan. Russian fur traders discovered the sea otter in 1741. Soon, the animal's fur became one of the most valuable furs on the market. As a result, the sea otter population began to shrink. By the early 1900s, many people doubted that the sea otter would survive, even though it became one of the first animals to receive protection in 1911.

It wasn't until the mid-1930s that sea otters were once again sighted. By the 1940s, a few sea otter populations near the Alaskan coast were reported to be outgrowing their habitat. A few groups were also found off the coast of California. During the 1950s and 1960s, the sea otter population was reported to be about 50,000, most of them in Alaska. This ongoing growth was a triumph for conservationists. Unfortunately, it also brought the sea otter into conflict with fishermen, who claim the otter ravages shellfish beds.

The sea otter is the smallest marine mammal, but it has a big appetite. It must constantly groom its fur to keep the fur from matting and losing its insulating qualities. To keep up this constant grooming, the sea otter requires a lot of food. Although a large sea otter weighs only about 100 pounds, it consumes nearly 25 pounds of food a day. What's more, the sea otter loves abalone, clams, and mussels, which also happen to be favorite meals of many humans.

While many fishermen think of the sea otter as a rival, many people marvel at the animal's antics. The sea otter lives in shallow waters so that it can dive to the bottom to collect shellfish. As it swims, it

Above: To open a clam shell, the sea otter first wraps itself in kelp to keep from drifting. Then, with a rock resting on its tummy, it slams the shell against the rock. **Right:** The sea otter's well-groomed fur is its only protection from the cold. If the fur becomes heavily soiled, the sea otter can quickly freeze to death.

stores food in a pouch that extends from under its leg to across its chest. When the sea otter returns to the surface, it floats on its back to dine. Observers are amazed when they watch the sea otter use a stone to break open the shells of its prey. This use of a "tool" is highly unusual in the animal kingdom.

The female sea otter is very protective of her newborn pup. The pup is totally dependent on its mother for food and grooming. While the mother dives for food, the pup floats on the surface. It is held afloat by a layer of air under its fur. This may be the only time in the sea otter's life when it is truly at risk from wild predators. On the other hand, even adult sea otters can fall victim to oil spills and other accidents.

To help the sea otter, conservationists have been moving groups of sea otters to other locations. This way, if another oil spill should occur, the entire population would not be destroyed. Conservationists also hope that by managing the sea otter population carefully, they will be able to reduce some of the tension between fishermen and sea otters. Through such efforts, perhaps the recovery of the sea otter may one day be complete.

Sea otters are playful creatures. A popular game among the species is to toss a stone down into the water, then dive under to catch it as it sinks.

HUMPBACK WHALE

If life-forms on another planet ever listen to the recordings on the Voyager I space explorer, one of the sounds they'll hear is the eerie "song" of the humpback whale. The enchanting songs and acrobatic feats of the humpback have captivated people for years.

The humpback's song consists of a long series of sounds that are repeated in the same order. The songs appear to be produced by males during the breeding season. Each group of humpbacks has a different song, and the songs vary from year to year. If these songs *are* mating calls, they are very unusual in the animal kingdom, because no other species appears to vary its mating call in this way.

The humpback is a baleen whale. Instead of teeth, it has long, thin, bonelike plates, called baleen, in its mouth. These plates allow it to strain food out of the water. The humpback is quite large, reaching an adult length of about 62 feet and an adult weight of about 53 tons. It is black in color, with a white or

speckled belly. It has long grooves on its throat and chest. Its flippers are long—about one third the body length—and have white undersides.

Biologists believe there are three separate geographical groups, or populations, of humpbacks—North Pacific, North Atlantic, and Southern Hemisphere. These groups do not appear to mix. Most humpbacks feed only in the summer, which they spend in colder waters. They eat plankton, sardines, mackerel, anchovies, and other small fish. During winter months, they migrate to warmer waters to breed. During the migration, they live on reserves of body fat. Biologists believe that the humpback migrates to allow the infant whale to be born in warmer waters, where it is easier for it to survive. Newborns, or calves, are about 13 to 14 feet long. The mothers nurse their young and are very protective. By the time the young whale is weaned at seven months, it may be more than 26 feet long.

Above: To dive deep into the ocean, the humpback whale hunches its back and rolls forward, flipping its huge tail straight up into the air. **Right:** Humpback whales must come to the surface of the ocean to breathe. The female humpback gives birth under water, then pushes her calf to the surface to get its first breath.

Like other marine mammals, the humpback must come to the surface of the ocean to breathe. The humpback can dive for up to 30 minutes before coming up for air. Within a few seconds of surfacing, the humpback can exhale nearly all the air in its lungs through two blowholes, or nostrils, on the top of its head. This results in the tall, thin "blow" observed by whale watchers. Unfortunately, this blow also helped whalers to spot and kill the humpback for its meat and oil until the species was near extinction.

It wasn't until 1946 that whalers began to regulate their kills. And it

wasn't until 1970 that eight whale species, including the humpback, were listed as endangered. Only the bowhead whale and the right whale are thought to be more severely threatened than the humpback. It is believed that about 10,000 humpbacks exist, but this estimate may be too optimistic.

Despite a ban on commercial whaling by the International Whaling Commission, the population of humpback whales appears to be decreasing. While no country allows the killing of humpbacks, the whales are but one of many victims of huge drift nets used for commercial fishing. Drift nets are between 25 and 50 feet deep and up to 40 miles long. They are almost invisible and appear to snag whatever comes their way. When the whales become trapped in the nets, they suffocate because they can't reach the surface to breathe. These nets have been outlawed by the United States government, but they are still used by Japanese and Korean fishing boats in international waters.

Conservationists are also concerned about the whale's environment. Increased pollution and decreases in the food supply in the whale's feeding grounds may make it more difficult for the remaining humpbacks to survive. In addition, some people fear that humans may be "loving" the whales too much. The wonderful acrobatics of the humpback attract more and more "whale-watching" boat tours to the whale's feeding and breeding grounds. There is some fear that the increase in noise will interfere with communication among the whales. One solution has been to create sanctuaries in the whale's breeding grounds, where boats are not allowed. Some sanctuaries have been created off the coasts of Hawaii. Further research may also help biologists find out if we can do more to prevent the day when a recording of the humpback's song is all that is left of this majestic creature.

With its winglike flippers and its ability to leap out of the water and spin (called breaching), the humpback is one of the most acrobatic whales in the ocean.

FLORIDA MANATEE

Manatees are very unusual marine mammals. Although they don't look at all like cows, people often call them "sea cows" because they "graze" on aquatic vegetation as they swim through warm, shallow coastal waters.

The manatee has been at home in the sea for 60 million years. The adult manatee is between ten and 13 feet long. It has a broad head and a flattened tail. It has no back limbs, and its front limbs are more like flippers than paws. Its skin color can be brown or gray, and it is hairless, except for the whiskers around its nose. The female manatee, called a cow, gives birth to one calf every two or three years. The calf stays in close contact with its mother for one to two years.

Manatees live in both fresh and salt water. Because they feed only in shallow water, they are never found far from land. All three species of manatees—the West African, the Amazonian, and the West Indian—are decreasing in numbers. There are small groups of West Indian manatees scattered along the tropical coasts of the Atlantic Ocean. They range from the southeastern United States to northern South America. The Amazonian manatee, which mainly inhabits the Amazon River in South America, is very endangered but is still killed for its meat. The West African manatee can be found in the rivers of tropical areas of West Africa. A related mammal, the dugong, is found in the Indian Ocean and nearby waters. These groups all belong to the same order of mammals, the Sirenia, although they do not mix.

Above: Called "sea cows" because they graze on seaweed and river plants, manatees have a split upper lip that allows them to grasp freshwater and saltwater plants. **Right:** The sight of the manatee, which floats upright in water, sparked tales of mermaids—fabled sea creatures that have the upper body of a woman and the tail of a fish.

In the United States, the Florida coasts are home to about 1,200 manatees. These Florida manatees are considered a subspecies of the West Indian manatees. The population is about evenly divided between the eastern and western coasts of Florida. This is as far north as manatees venture, because they cannot survive in cold waters. Even Florida manatees seek warmer water during the winter. If the winter is unusually cold,

manatee deaths can be relatively high. For example, during the winter of 1989-90, unusually cold weather struck Florida. As a result, 65 manatees were found dead.

Conservationists are hoping to save the Florida manatee from the fate of its relative, the Steller sea cow. The Stellar sea cow was the only member of the Sirenia order that had adapted to cold northern waters. It was hunted to extinction in the 18th century.

Manatees are completely protected in the United States. They are no longer killed here for their meat. The population is still endangered, however, because manatees continue to die from accidental injuries. Many of Florida's manatees have scars on their backs from boat propellers. Most manatee deaths are caused by collisions with boats, barges, and floodgates.

The Florida manatee's survival depends greatly on the behavior and attitudes of people. By obeying boat speeds in manatee areas, boaters can reduce the chance that a manatee will be killed in a collision. Such deaths can also be reduced by limiting the development of marinas in manatee feeding areas.

Biologists are also trying to learn more about the manatee in the hopes of increasing its chances for survival. For example, an increasing number of manatee calves have been dying in recent years. No one knows why. Biologists hope to determine if human activity affects manatee reproduction. They also want to know if the manatee is being harmed by pollution in its feeding grounds. Increased algae growth can kill the vegetation on which the manatee feeds. Biologists hope that a combination of scientific study and protection can help the manatee avoid the fate of its cousin, the Steller sea cow.

Manatee calves stay close to their mother for one to two years after birth. Manatees communicate with each other by rubbing muzzles. When frightened, they squeak.

GREEN SEA TURTLE

The sea turtle is one of the most mysterious creatures in the world. While we know some things about this giant reptile, there are still many aspects of its life and behavior that we don't understand. For example, we know that this reptile spends most of its life in the ocean. But we don't know how it manages to stay under water for an hour before coming up for air. We also know that the sea turtle returns to land only to lay its eggs. But why does it return to the same beach where it was born to lay its eggs? And how does it find its way there across thousands of miles? By saving the sea turtle from extinction, biologists hope to find the answers to these mysteries.

The green sea turtle is one of six kinds of giant sea turtles found in United States waters that are protected under the Endangered Species Act. It lives in warm-water regions all over the world. In the United States, most of its nesting areas are on the east coast of Florida.

On nesting day, the female turtle comes ashore. Her forelimbs look like paddles. They are much better suited to swimming than crawling, so her journey across the sand is very difficult. She struggles to reach land that is safe for her eggs. Once there, she uses her rear flippers to dig a big hole. She then lays about 100 eggs. People watching the sea turtle lay her eggs often think that she's crying. Actually, she's getting rid of the salt in her body through ducts near her eyes.

Once her eggs are laid and covered with sand, she must once again make the long journey back across the sand. Some females die if they can't get to the ocean fast enough, because the sun quickly dries out their shells.

About 50 days later, the eggs hatch, and the hatchlings rush to the sea. Many of the hatchlings are eaten by predators before they reach the water. Others are eaten by fish once they get into the water. The turtles that survive into adulthood have few natural enemies in the

Above: Named for the color of its fat, the green sea turtle can measure up to three feet in length and weigh up to 400 pounds. It eats jellyfish, marine grasses, fish, mollusks, and other sea creatures. **Right:** The female green sea turtle struggles across the sand to lay her eggs on the same beach where she was born. The male waits offshore.

animal world. But for thousands of years, humans have been killing turtles, eating their meat and eggs, and using their shells to make ornaments.

Long ago, people began to notice that giant sea turtles were disappearing. Almost 300 years ago, the killing of young turtles was banned in Bermuda, an island in the Caribbean. Today, many things are being done to save the green sea turtle. Along the coasts of Florida, fences are set up to protect the turtles and their eggs. Human activity has been restricted in some nesting areas. And along some

beaches in Florida, the use of artificial lights is restricted during nesting times, because these lights can confuse the turtles.

In other countries, eggs are moved to special heated boxes to protect them from animals and people until the baby turtles are ready to hatch. The eggs are then returned to the beach so that when the young turtles grow up, they will know where to return to lay their eggs.

Shrimp nets are also a major problem for the turtles. A sea turtle must come to the surface for air. If it gets trapped in a shrimp net, it can drown. So Turtle Excluder Devices, called TEDs, are required on all shrimp boats off Cape Canaveral. These devices allow the turtles to escape from the nets. But shrimp fishermen say TEDs also allow much of their catch to escape. The Department of Commerce is trying to require TEDs in all offshore waters of the southeast United States.

Sea turtles are also threatened by oil slicks and other water pollution. Plastic trash carelessly tossed into the ocean can kill a turtle. To a turtle, a piece of plastic floating on the water may look like its favorite food, jellyfish. When the turtle swallows the plastic, it can choke to death. So, by helping to keep the oceans clean, you may be able to save a green sea turtle's life.

The green sea turtle has been hunted nearly to extinction for its meat and eggs. Turtle soup—long considered to be a delicacy in many countries—is made from this species.

AMERICAN CROCODILE

When you think of crocodiles, do you picture them living in African jungles? Well, you might be surprised to discover that one of the world's largest crocodiles is the American crocodile. Most American crocodiles live in the swamps of Central and South America. A few, however, live in the southern part of Florida on a narrow string of islands called the Florida Keys.

Most people can't tell the difference between the American crocodile and the American alligator, another large reptile that lives in Florida. Both have a long, lizardlike body, four short limbs, and a powerful tail. In both species, the eyes are on the top of the skull. This allows them to see as they cruise near the surface of the water looking for food. They both come on land to sun themselves, build nests, and lay their eggs.

There are, however, a few physical differences between the two reptiles. The alligator is slightly smaller than the crocodile, which can grow to a length of 20 feet. The American

crocodile's long snout tapers to a point, while the alligator's snout is more rounded. Also, the fourth tooth on either side of the crocodile's lower jaw is visible when its mouth is closed. Of course, most of us wouldn't want to get close enough to see the differences between crocodiles and alligators. Both reptiles can be very dangerous. But while many people have spotted alligators in Florida, few people have seen the American crocodile, because it is very rare, especially in the United States.

One main reason that the American crocodile is endangered is that it was hunted for many years. The crocodile's skin was used to make a variety of items, including belts, shoes, and purses. Today, however, the American crocodile is protected in the United States. It is illegal to kill them or to buy or sell their skins. Many other countries also have laws that forbid the buying or selling of crocodile skins. In certain countries, such as Australia, crocodiles are raised on

Above: The crocodile has a powerful bite, but the muscles that open the jaw are not very strong. A man can hold the reptile's mouth closed using just his hands. **Right:** Despite their reputations, most crocodiles very rarely attack people. Indeed, the American crocodile is so rare that few people in the United States have ever seen one.

farms, and their skins are then harvested. This is done in the hope that people will leave the wild crocodiles alone. In some cases, so many crocodiles are produced on the farms that the farmers release the extra crocodiles into the wild.

The other reason that the American crocodile is endangered is because most of its swampy habitat is being lost to farming and development. This is especially true in highly populated places like Florida, where many swamps have been drained and replaced by farms and housing developments. Without swamps, the American crocodile will not survive.

The American crocodile may appear ugly and unfriendly, but it plays an important role in the balance of nature by eating fish and small animals. To get its fill of fish and turtles, the crocodile moves its muzzle sideways and scoops up its prey. Although the crocodile has excellent vision above the water, its sight gets blurry underwater. So, it's likely that the crocodile catches underwater prey by sensing movement. To catch land animals, the crocodile floats motionless near the water's edge until its prey approaches. The reptile then uses its powerful tail to knock the animal into the water. Its sharp teeth look dangerous, but actually the crocodile cannot chew that well. It uses its teeth to grab its prey, and then drowns it. The crocodile then stores the prey under logs or tree roots to eat later.

You may think that the crocodile's hunting habits sound cruel. Without the crocodile, however, these small animals and fish might become too numerous and might outgrow their food supplies. Eventually, many of these creatures might die of starvation. So, the American crocodile has its own unique place in the food chain.

American alligators have been protected for a long time. Their numbers are increasing throughout their range in the southeastern United States. Conservationists hope that by protecting American swamplands, the American crocodile can be saved as well.

This newly hatched American crocodile is about nine inches long. The female crocodile lays her eggs in the sand and then stands guard over them. When the eggs are ready to hatch, she digs them out so the hatchlings can breathe. To keep her young safe once they have hatched, she may carry them in her mouth.

CALIFORNIA CONDOR

For a long time, people have been arguing about how to save the California condor. More than 100 years ago, scientists knew that it was disappearing from the wild. Despite many attempts to save this huge bird, its survival is still in question. Today, fewer than 40 birds survive, and all of them are in captivity. The California condor's last hope is that man can learn how to increase the number of condors, teach them how to survive in the wild, and protect them so that they can live free.

The California condor is the largest bird in the United States. From wingtip to wingtip, it measures up to nine feet across. Unlike most birds, it doesn't feed on insects and seeds. It is a vulture, which means that it feeds on the meat of dead animals, called carrion. The condor can live to be 50 years old, and the species as a whole has been on earth for a very long time. Biologists believe that, in the ice age, the condor fed off the dead bodies of mammals like the wooly

mammoth, which has been extinct for millions of years.

At one time, California condors flew across all of North America. By the time the California condor was classified as a species more than 150 years ago, scientists already knew that its population was decreasing. It had been hunted for many years. The nest areas of the California condor had been disturbed by settlers. And many of the birds had died of lead poisoning after eating the meat of animals that had been killed with lead bullets.

In the 1930s, scientists believed there were only 70 birds left, all of them living in a small, mountainous area of southern California. Fortunately for the condor, researchers did not ignore this bird. A zoologist named Carl Koford began to study the bird. His research led the United States Forest Service to establish a condor sanctuary. Many other projects were begun to help save the condor, but its population continued to shrink.

Above: California condors soared through the skies for many hundreds of years. They were even around during the ice age. Today, fewer than 40 survive, and all are in captivity. **Right:** The California condor is mostly black in color, with a bare yellow head, an orange-red neck, and white linings in its wings.

In 1979, the Federal Fish and Wildlife Service established a plan to capture all the surviving condors and put tags on them. Some would then be released in the wild. Others would be kept in captivity to form a breeding colony. This plan was opposed by many groups, mostly because they thought too many birds would die during the capture. These groups also felt that if all the birds were captured, people would no longer want to protect condor habitat. If the habitat disappeared, the bird could never be returned to the wild. Even after the plan was put into effect, the debate continued.

By 1983, the captive population was increased to nine birds. By this time, biologists had learned how to successfully raise the chicks that hatched in captivity. Their keepers wore hand puppets that looked like condors, so that the chicks would become familiar with their own species. That way, when the chicks matured, they would be able to recognize other California condors and find a mate. This proved to be very lucky, because many of the remaining condors in the wild were dying. Again, wildlife protection groups were divided over a new plan to bring all the condors into captivity in an effort to save the species.

In 1987, the last wild condor was captured. The entire captive population, less than 40 birds, is now divided between the San Diego Wild Animal Park and the Los Angeles Zoo, both in California. Biologists hope they can breed enough condors so that some can be released into the wild. To prepare for that step, biologists have been working with the Andean condor, a very close relative of the California condor. A group of female Andean condors was released in southern California so that researchers could study how the birds readapt to the wild. If the experiment with the Andean condors is successful, and if the number of captive California condors can be increased, the next step will be to release some of the captive California condors. Biologists hope to carry out this plan between 1993 and 1995. If successful, a condor refuge in the Los Padres National Forest in southern California may once again be the home of wild California condors.

The California condor is one of the heaviest birds in the world. Yet, if the wind is right, the condor can soar for nearly ten miles without having to flap its wings.

WHOOPING CRANE

The graceful whooping crane, with its long, white neck, is special for two reasons. It stands about five feet high—that's taller than most children—making it America's tallest bird. It is also special because it is so rare. Indeed, the whooping crane is one of the rarest birds in the world.

Like many marsh birds, the whooping crane has long legs for wading through shallow water. Unlike many other kinds of birds, it never perches in trees. It makes its nest on the ground. It is called the whooping crane because of the loud, trumpeting sound it makes. It is white, with black feet, black trim on its wings, and a red face. Its wingspan, measuring from one wingtip to the other, is more than seven feet.

Whooping cranes are migrating birds. Their winter feeding ground is in Texas. In the spring, they fly thousands of miles north to Canada to nest. There, the female cranes lay their eggs. The chicks hatch in about a month. When the young

birds are about four months old, they take off with their parents for the south again.

Compared to most birds, the whooping crane population was probably always small. The female whooping crane lays only two eggs a year, and the parents raise only one chick. The second chick usually dies because it is not strong enough to compete for the food provided by the parents. Whooping cranes eat a variety of reptiles, frogs, insects, and plants. But each pair of birds requires a huge range—usually about 300 to 400 acres—in which to hunt.

Despite its relatively small population, the whooping crane could once be found on the Great Plains and the Atlantic and Gulf coasts of the United States, as well as in central Mexico. When Europeans arrived in North America, however, the birds started to disappear. The whooping crane lost much of its range to farms and towns. Because of the bird's huge size, it was an easy target for

Above: With a wingspan of more than seven feet, the whooping crane can travel through the skies at a rate of more than 40 miles per hour. **Right:** Scientists estimate that whoopers have lived on the North American continent for at least 500,000 years. Conservationists are working to ensure that the birds are around for many more.

hunters. Even the bird's eggs were easily collected, because the whooping crane nests on the ground. Given that there weren't many whooping cranes to begin with, it seemed that the whooping crane didn't have a chance to survive.

In 1941, biologists believed there were only 16 whooping cranes left in the world. These birds were found in a coastal swamp in Texas, where they fed in the winter and mated in the spring. But no one knew where the birds went to nest and hatch their eggs. It took 13 years for scientists to discover the birds'

summer home in Wood Buffalo National Park in Canada. It seemed that the whooping crane had managed to find one place where it could survive beyond the threats of man. Once found, this last flock of rare birds got quite a bit of help from conservationists.

For many years, it has been illegal to kill whooping cranes, take their eggs, or disturb their nests. The Texas winter feeding ground was made into a protected area, called the Aransas National Wildlife Refuge. In addition, scientists tried a unique experiment designed to help increase the whooping crane population. The scientists had discovered that a similar bird, the sandhill crane, would hatch the eggs of the whooping crane and raise the young birds. As mentioned previously, adult whooping cranes can only nurture one of the two baby cranes born after each mating. The other one generally dies. So, the scientists removed one egg from many of the whooping crane nests in Canada and placed them in sandhill crane nests. Not only were the eggs hatched, but the sandhill cranes became "foster parents" for the newly hatched whoopers. The program has been cancelled, however, because scientists discovered that, for some reason, these adopted whoopers have not been able to reproduce.

Still, the efforts to protect the whooping crane and its habitat have paid off. The number of whooping cranes continues to grow. In 1989, 146 whooping cranes made the 2,500-mile journey between Texas and Canada. This was an increase of eight cranes over the previous year. Today, the whooping crane population is estimated to be over 200. While the population is still very small, and thus very vulnerable, the rescue of the whooping crane provides a glimmer of hope to those who are fighting to save other endangered species from extinction.

At mating time, the male whooper begins the "courtship dance" by bowing to the female. The female then joins in. The dance consists of bows, leaps, sways, and whoops.

GLOSSARY

aquatic: living or growing in water

breeding colony: a collection of animals of the same species that are brought together, usually in captivity, to reproduce

captive breeding: the taking of animals out of the wild for the express purpose of bringing them together to reproduce. Captive breeding is one method used to increase the population of species that are rare or endangered.

carnivore: an animal that eats flesh. The order of mammals called *Carnivora* includes dogs, cats, bears, seals, and weasels.

carrion: the decaying flesh of dead animals

CITES: Convention of International Trade in Endangered Species of Wild Fauna and Flora. A treaty signed by more than 100 countries around the world. The member nations agree not to sell or trade endangered animals or their parts. They also agree to manage threatened and protected species by regulating trade in the animals and their parts.

conservationist: a person who supports or aids in the protection and wise use of natural resources, such as wildlife

endangered species: a species that is in danger of being wiped out, or becoming extinct, in all or a large part of its range. In the United States, animals that have "endangered species" status are protected under the Endangered Species Act. *See* Endangered Species Act

Endangered Species Act: a federal law that requires the United States government to identify animals that are in danger of being wiped out. The Act makes it illegal to buy or sell endangered animals (or their parts, such as fur or horns) or products made from them. It also requires government agencies to take a look, beforehand, at how new government projects may affect wildlife habitat. In addition, the Act requires the government to make a list of "threatened" animals, or animals that may soon become endangered.

extinction: the dying out of a species of animals or plants

habitat: the natural place in which an animal normally lives, grows, and finds food and cover

herbivore: an animal that eats plants

marine: of or relating to the sea or ocean

migration: the act of moving regularly from one area or climate to another in order to feed or breed

omnivore: an animal that eats both plants and flesh

poaching: the act of hunting, killing, or taking wildlife illegally

predator: an animal that hunts another animal for food

prey: an animal that is hunted by another animal for food

protected: refers to the legal measures taken to help prevent a threatened or endangered species from being wiped out. In the United States, animals that are given "endangered species" status by the government are protected under the Endangered Species Act (*see* Endangered Species Act). Legal measures used to defend "threatened" animals may not be as extensive (*see* threatened).

range: the area in which an animal is naturally found

refuge/reserve/sanctuary: areas of land, both public and private, used for the protection and wise use of wildlife

species: a group of related animals that look like one another and that are able to breed with one another and produce offspring that can breed. Members of one species do not usually breed with members of another.

subspecies: a group of animals within a species that show minor local variations. Often, the term is used when separate populations of a species are found in different geographical areas.

threatened species: a species that is likely, in the near future, to become endangered in part or all of its usual range. In the United States, animals that are given "threatened species" status by the government are usually afforded some protection. For example, tightly controlled hunting of a threatened animal may be allowed. The number of "kills" allowed may be limited. Steps such as these are often taken to help manage "problem" animals within a species (*see* grizzly bear *profile, for example*) while helping to prevent the species as a whole from being wiped out.